Words for the Music Nobody Listens to

no supplicant arts your dreadful rage control

ORPHEUS

November 14 plus 5th returned from the house of the dead just when the stopped clock told the right time at 3.17. I wound it up. Snow had fallen heavily on the night previous, but the sun shone now.

FROM THE DIARY OF ENVER GAMMUL

John Smith

MindMyBunionPress
John Smith © 2025
All Rights Reserved
ISBN:978-1739327330

CONTENTS

VERSE	5
INDEX OF FIRST LINES	40
DETATCHED TITLES	44

1

The world ended last night
and the winged exciseman is collecting
his final demand for earthly debt,
while the all-consuming worm,
defrauded, starves in the bone yard
and the audience mummifies
in front breakfast-time TV,
but some people get up and carry on
just like they always did before,
you see, the sun always shone
for them paler than the moon
and flesh was never the fashion.
They already led spectral lives
and maybe you are one of them.

2

The prim whores, the countless labouring drones,
all too typical of too many dormitory towns,
the massed ranks of the hopelessly bland,
their births were welcomed, often planned,
no thanks to yet-one-more crappy doctor,
except, perhaps, it was him that cocked her,
but some were born to ruin the neighbourhood,
so when the news said, 'One's dead.' The rest said,
'Good!'
'But think, John! Maternity ward! A genius! Like out of
thin air!'
Let's see …
No, not this year, the vintage is ALL *vin ordinaire*.

3

Allow me to tell you, to your myriad faces,
about the world's most sterile places:
the sad sultan's realms of gold,
the palaces where stifling dreams unfold,
or this, under the shining winds,
the land of silver mountains
where the fat, flippered cattle
mew, weep and prattle
at the edge of endless white miles,
and there the Ice King smiles
and murmurs into his wine –
'Mine.'
For such grandeur battles are won, and lost,
then in the fire, or the frost,
triumphant princes must ask the wizard's advice,
How to live amongst icicles, or lice?
Their reply is the same, 'No faithful kiss
'supplants the serpent's bliss.
'to find the most pleasure – murder the dear.
'Usurp birth,' they say, 'and other things rear.
'They too may also break the heart,
'but they keep keen the itchy part
'fostering that which in prison minds teem –
'cock in a harem;
'for, Lord, within the armour of misery
'swelters the sharpest ecstasy.'

4

All are types and each is loved
by someone, somewhere – **** ** **** shoved,
and these simple bodily jerks
are how love works,
so just keep fucking while you live,
God will not condemn, or forgive.

5

Adam and his Siamese twin, Eve
had a long, difficult stillbirth yesterday,
they named the foetus Mo—, no, Jes—, no, *Steve*.
He's here! *Pate foie gras* on the tray.
"Brrrrrrrap!" Adam muses via his rectal organ,
"Say you now the fruits of sin are so sparse?"
(Eve vomits more juice on the *****,
Adam tears a new page and wipes his arse.)
*********, ***** and a billion ******
bend and blow out the smiling sun,
Mother-earth worshippers bugger kangaroos,
atheists are the onanists who spurt and run,
now our souls lick shit out of jakes and loos
for all eternity – and eternity's just begun.

6

Not born deformed, to grovel in a chair?
Not mad, stupid, or otherwise unaware?
Then put up with strong and weak
and watch vileness pile to a peak
on which sits a head of tinsel and glitter,
call it God, it could not be fitter,
for look at humans, tall and hollow,
all of them demanding that all should follow,
look at the evidence in films, books and plays,
the one fact any culture displays,
that two emotions fill our earthly state –
self love, and its Siamese twin – hate.

7

I see the future in electric cables
stretched across a gray, yet restless sky,
I feel reality, stripped of human labels,
standing at the window, as if to pry…
but there's nothing to see,
it's Sunday, in the afternoon I sleep,
forget yesterday's impropriety,
and wake up when an actress begins to weep
on the set next door. I switch mine on
to watch and wearily mock each extreme,
sex, money, pretend hero and demon –
society on the latrine.
I see the future as monkeys
pushing buttons for a fuck,
a machine and its lackeys,
nothing really worth a look.

8

The universe is a dirty plaster wall,
paradise a potted geranium, grey and stale,
God sweeps high above the lino floor –
a severed head swung from a rusty nail.
Behold! The ocean is a single, squirming fish,
the sun is the moon, all hot and feverish,
the wind – an almighty sneeze of flu,
the forest – a tree that never grew,
the desert is a single grain of sand,
and Man is this thing, a part-dissected gland,
as illustrated in *The Anatomy of the Ass*
the one true holy book. Now, as planned,
the oven opens – the Prophet breathes gas.

9

You ask, *What are these days?* These are the last days,
hours and hours of fitful news summaries
of what happened in last week's foggy haze,
or a morning spent recalling the mummeries
of youth acted out in city beds,
or months of medical tomfooleries
internet-searched to shreds.
And now for the law, forged into the nonsense
that makes our words not what we mean
and we are ever less credible in consequence,
until the terminal fall of self esteem
during the calamity of an unforeseen gale
that knocks L-shapes off the windscreen
with knuckle bones of final hail.

10

Noticed everything is held together by loosening screws
these days? And infirm joints and uncertain sinews?
Yes, yes, there are all sorts of epochs
that come to an end when someone knocks
and a doctor, or a mechanic meets our eyes.
They say, 'We must find someone who still supplies,
'the part that is needed, it may take, perhaps, a week,
'but call straight away if there's a blockage, or leak.
'In the meantime, it's the law, I must do as directed
'and fix this label, right here.' *Must Stay Disconnected.*

11

These things in our heads aren't memories,
they are what media execs use to fill screen slots,
they are the by-products of high-tech industries
breaking reality down into tiny little dots.
The majority of people today are media mirages,
so how can we trust our next prophet or messiah?
What about a dog, whelped behind garages
on a run-down estate? No dog could be a liar!
and a talking dog – that'd prove there's a God.
He'd say, "You are blind – I'll show the way."
His lead will guide you down the path he trod,
and if he turns fanatical – just shout, "Stay!"

12

Exotic animals in cages
can reach impressive ages,
because advanced agriculture
feeds the snake and vulture
to stay still and stay in view
so that a return might accrue,
but really, movies do much better,
their two dimensions fetter
the most multifarious beast
to fuck for us, or die at least.

13

What use the moon when this world frowns?
What hope when a chant of abstract nouns
seeps from the warehouse? What is this law
that rules the mind as carpet rules the floor
and denies there can be any excuse
because day dreams have gone out of use?
How soon subtle thoughts fall apart.
How little is left to art
in a vast, self canceling spawn
of minds full of sport and porn.
With the advent of clock winding death,
lugging his swag bag at the very last breath,
is the management defrauded of its power?
No, new breeds are ten-a-penny, by-the-hour,
new proles, new bosses too, with the age-old flaw
of not knowing they're of no use at all.

14

So many, so many, like leaves of trees
moved by some thin little breeze
who fall and join generations of mold,
the history of which is nothing to be told,
no matter how noble, how obscene,
for what could our history ever mean
to whomever eternity is a minute,
to He who made the world and put sin in it,
for He will turn this world, or turn it not,
let it freeze, or, if warm, let it rot,
to Him the good, the bad, the utter waste,
the living, the dead, they're all to his taste.

15

This is the night where my heart longs to quicken,
this is the light that my word will thicken,
I will tear up clay and whittle stones
and join the two as flesh and bones
and shocked by touch and left to swarm
there will be lust of every form,
then, to learn whether I exist at all,
I will listen out for the grammatical,
otherwise I will rest – perhaps forever more,
content if they name me and call,
'Redeem us and raise us on the final day.'
And, you know, I just may.

16

We wake and our good or bad dreams
fall and drop away, collapsed scenes
in an empty theatre, the show that closed
after the first night. And it must be supposed
that, in the end, the props of the happy life,
career, kids and a wonderful wife
will one day count the same as bad luck,
the disappointments and the muck
of failure. 'Mere painted gimcrack,'
we'll say – if we wake. Ah, that's the knack,
to wake, although the cheapest show up town
(our life), quite rightly, has closed down.

17

Dawn, and they sound so overjoyed,
lately returned from the chilly void,
whence they conveyed the souls of the dead,
an undertaking they nowise dread.
The long journey, by wing, is brief,
so light, they cannot be touched by grief,
ever cheerful in their grave office
to leave our souls in realms of ice.
Morning is a melodious thing,
listen, how gaily the song birds sing,
Recall those who balled down the day?
Rejoice, we have flown the lot away!

18

Whenever you are told
to go straight to the house of the dead
because you are old,
just you go back-to-front instead,
then you will arrive
clearly looking all set to leave,
backwards alive.
to hear the mourners grieve
for you in the shades
never believing you could backslide,
but their light fades,
not yours, when death goes cross-eyed.

19

The banana falls not far from the banana tree
and provokes no ideas on astronomy,
in fact, no thoughts at all come to pass
while breakfast moves from mouth to ass.

Down, down into the underworld of drains,
up, up to nose and then to brains,
this miasma, as in little muddy puddles,
produces thoughts in tiny little bubbles.

Snout up high, IQ low,
prank the bongo, 'Go monkey go,'
they cry, I say, banana go and rot
and end these days of idiot.

20

Despite the brooding clouds saying who knows what,
despite the pain and shame finally forgot,
despite joyous birdsong, albeit brief at dawn,
despite blooms, spontaneous in the lawn,
despite Mister W. not burning Mister H.'s verse
despite the lifting of every lifelong curse,
despite venerable abode and new acres of sun,
there are holes through which life must run.

21

Most odd that it's from the world atomic,
of all the known worlds the most laconic,
they squeeze out the power invisible
to send the face and voice most risible
of booming cannibals, of hissing ghouls
to countless screens gawped at by countless fools.
May that morning come, when it will be found
that birdsong alone is the loudest sound,
when the evergreens will end their retreat
and smother the lot, street by grubby street.

22

God help me, I want a war
to scatter the foe like straw.
Sweep, Holy Scythe, make stalks bleed,
sever contaminate seed.
Swill the gutter, Lord, soak the field,
annihilate and paradise yield …
I cannot otherwise adore,
God help me, I want a war.

24

Give to the King of the Dead
not to the starving instead,
waste no hallowed hymns
on balloon bellies and stick limbs.
Our fields must lie fallow,
famine must slim their marrow,
then vainly the flutes of bone
sing hollow, *You must atone,*
for we forge, rather than mourn,
forge arms that glitter by morn.
O charity, you must learn to fast,
we have our destiny, at last,
and more to atom and to virus
our debt. Your dearth pays for us.
So abominated, not fed,
hail you the King of the Dead.

22

Our aim was swift and true
ten millennia ago,
we ran the beast right through,
till every land rang hollow.

Bloated bellies soon supplied
new flesh, monkey faced,
so many starved and cried,
yet death was out-paced.

The yammering pimp's snout,
the squeal of its bored whore,
please sick this headache out!
Hear, dear God, I long for war.

Oh, because your aim is true,
ten millennia from now,
trust me, you will run yourself through
till every land rings hollow.

23

What a world of amity
cleansed of humanity.
Enemies now abound,
by the kind condoned,
be good, these plead
and they duly breed,
on and on it will go
till the corpse will blow.
The children crawl, then fly
and blot out the sky.
Charity asks we care,
demands too we share
to feed the enemy.
Everyone else, not me!
For that's the opposite
of the cure of it.
With that power to realise
I will do otherwise,
after Armageddon,
tend home and garden.

24

Behold the monsters, on the street,
below the stairs, overhead, under feet,
but human, of course, as you and me,
but fucking monkeys, just off the tree,
to look at them is to feel I am not,
and to pray, "*Alien Hero*, kill the lot!"

25

Let all the graveyards join into one,
let the rest in pitch dark become undone.
Hail new world, fit for sparrows, mice and frogs,
sing friends, no more monkeys, or Gods.
See the garden of stones and yew
oak lids for tables, lead baths for dew.
So dine and bathe and live ever more,
while the universe goes to dust and straw.

26

To converse with them is hardly worthwhile,
they who yet live will but sour and spoil,
one might expect to hear and feel more
by rapping on a sepulchre door.
So go visiting, as did those romancers,
the old beaux known as necromancers,
debouch in boudoirs of oak and lead
to talk with and, indeed, love the dead.

27

On the day the Earth stands still,
descend, robot mine, with that laser in your head,
and destroy the deity who deems it ill
that I live, let the *Holy Ghost* die instead.

Rise from the very deep and attack,
O titan monster, city by hostile city,
and heap up corpses in a stack,
all humanity reap, all except me.

The dawn is bright, toll the church bell,
for green ghoul and red-mouthed cannibal
are gone and along with them Hell,
now the Earth turns again and is wonderful.

28

Lord, it seems yours is the greater sway
among the citizenry of insects,
they are ten thousand per ounce of our clay
and each ranges far, and stings and infects,
an avenging angel to see that we pay
in pain and pus and rot for titan lust,
till only a jaw bone is left to pray,
level now with the fly and locust,
so if truly we were the beast to slay,
in plague, war and famine let us trust.

29

Turn the tap, fill the swimming pool with blood,
loose the hot air balloon stitched from skin,
bolt the bones and lift a tower in the wood,
light the candle fat now all are ghost-thin.

Turn the blood into black
and let it run into my page
so the verse will not lack
a curse for the present age.

30

Ah, a professional numerator,
planning to make concrete more complete,
importing a bigger lower denominator,
behold, more street, less wheat, same elite.
So the future will be the last of many fractions
of what the past used to be,
milliards of tin-pot father's sons,
just to keep this dullard busy.

31

Autobiography by non anon,
good if it's soon forgotten,
better if it's left half written,
best if it was never begun.
Well, good riddance then, someone.

32

Dear God, not yet another provincial bore,
a brain tumor cured, left with an odd eye,
a monster to look at, to hear, a chore!
'I've lived by my wits.' Oh window-pane fly!
It's on the tip of my tongue, *I just do not care.*
The big monster Man just splits and splits
and the little monsters get everywhere,
if only they died by their wits.

33

Let the flags of the future unfold and fold
and the wind whistle down the drain,
let the blue moon give the sun a cold
and let the past go from whence it came.

We saw snow fall on both bees and blossom,
we read the books that were lately unwritten,
we heard where profit takes a loss from,
we dreamed today never did happen.

So let the song tune out the singer,
let the trees put their leaves on hold,
let the receiver cancel the sender,
let the flags of the future unfold and fold.

34

God damn this overcrowded provincial hole.
I've just met the local intellectual
and in a conversation that took its toll
he said, 'Who's Kafka?' and 'I sit on the council.'

35

Hail prophet, whose prophecies have never dimmed,
hail bright spirit alighting on the tall poplar's top,
in love with the midday sun and the noon-time wind,
I ask this, 'How many summers before summers stop?'

He replies, 'Certain blooms, lets call them x, y and z
'Are growing at the feet of certain hereabout trees
'in the garden of the couple, now two winters dead
'and these will be visited by a number of bees.

'Last year for a certain span of days a street light shone,
'but never shone for half the hours on a certain night
'and in half that time so many Vs of geese have gone
'to the left of my head, others have gone to my right.

'The total times this summer the sirens sang,
'to the swooping notes on a femur flute,
'less the chimes for you, O thief, that never rang,
'are the days between your wedding and funeral suit.'

After four-fifths of a life, we thus converse
and I, a mortal, am much too quick
to require answers of him in chanted verse,
and hence received riddles in arithmetic.

36

The ivied-woodland ways, sacred to the moon,
that led to a hollow alter, brimming with blood,
into which corn new-born was strewn
by the cowled herald of death, or motherhood,
are buried by roads and cables laid athwart
to convey the paradise that we bought.

The lightening from the cloud's thick breast
once lit the monster's brass hands
that reached out to tear and wrest
gore from the beast into coiled ribbons,
now, in place of the lonely, single sacrifice,
hospitals light hecatombs of human mice.

Flesh is grass, but cannot fill the fields,
except the mind, disgusted, must reel
and the soul cry out for she who wields
the moonlit sickle of pious steel
and a holy holocaust, always the harshest,
to render Man meagre and full the harvest.

37

Last night the stars never shone so far away,
today revelation is closer by another day.
Here, some forgotten cause built this town,
somewhere else the walls fell down.
The head, a bulb of bone, is full of meat
for worms, while dogs gnaw crooked gristle, feet.
Today, the revelation has come and gone,
tonight, further have the stars never shone.

38

At the very last rank of quiescent night
the props are expectant in the barest light,
vehicles, ornaments, the kids' garden swing
are waiting for the actors to dance and sing.
Yet, despite the mega, sell-out performance,
the theatre's closed, the unforeseen circumstance
we always denied, but guessed must simply come
has come and the stage has fallen dark and dumb.
But as for the props, how will death impinge?
Will it stop the wind and the plaintive hinge?
If not, take heart, the props, now that we are gone,
may resume themselves, and sort of live on.

39

Trees and trees and trees will grow
along the ways the motorways go
and surely mankind must lose its drive,
since both cars and trees cannot thrive.
Now moss smothers the motorway signs
and all alone the lone moon shines,
but should sun and wind pluck the moss away
the signs, by any light, have nothing left to say.
Listen, ivy, much, still grows at journey's end,
so very much that the rooftops bend
and when, at last, the rain pours in,
there will be no chilly, shivering skin
and no corn at all in any field,
just the worms they always yield.

40

The hill resonates with arrows of geese
querying the words, *love* and *peace*,
with wings that drum the gunmetal sky,
the ghosts of those yet to die.

The resurrection is in flying ants,
enacted among faded summer plants
and the *Holy Spirits* fly on gossamer filaments
with which spiders weave their tenements.

The auguries have never been so clear
as seen in the beast immolated this year,
they say, *Pity blood, for only sap*
will rise again when the leaves unwrap.

41

We are surrounded by things that live at our command
and so it's rather ironic, you'll smile if you understand,
when we're powered down, let's say by a little cough,
there is no choice, we stay permanently switched off.

42

What else is Man? After the battle
they fashioned their bones into gates
and fences for grazing cattle,
hinged skeletons to squeak at the fates.
What else is Man? Heads as empty
as streetlamps on gray days,
soulless stalks after the past of plenty,
this is what the future says.

43

Look, nature is a host of fanatics,
adherents to the cult of mechanics,
small, frantic atoms, mighty molecules
who never break arithmetical rules,
thus, when we oscillate, become unsprung,
that never means the sums are wrong,
the balance of pleasure and pain
parallelograms can easily explain,
and think momentum and inertia
rather than diarrhoea and dementia,
while rheumatic joints, yes, they are a blight,
but their total stress can be gauged just right.
So, instead of God, a vague patrician,
blame Abbott, Percival, mathematician.

44

The drain gurgles through a rainy night
and knows what he says is only right,
Eat all those dead-soul eggs
and see your roots turned to legs.

Then the ash tree shivers in the wind
to hear he'll come over all loose limbed
and leave what fate decreed his place
to live new tales of time and space.

45

O citizens, in this age of ever more infectious crimes
head for CGI worlds and their centrally-heated climes,
but while the virus shows splendid ingenuity,
your fantasy films mirror ineffable banality,
those off-the-shelf monsters and heroic deeds
that soulless corps swill down broadband leads
whereby, in crowds, you dream you are individual,
then wake still more willingly illiberal.
How you hate my flesh, not inoculated,
and my mind no less, not indoctrinated,
confirmed by what you mutter behind a mask,
but deny it, wide eyed, when, 'You what?' I ask,
then indeed they grimace at my right to smile,
free of vaccine and, thank you light, free of bile.

46

There's crucial fish in our lavatory sea,
and below our feet, useful gas in shale,
there is more need, but less electricity,
there is a first name for every gale.

We shall gain friends when we take offence,
our sales will rise when our specie fades,
even the Prime Minister will make sense,
shouting over the racket of missile raids.

We'll make war out of generosity,
we'll flush our seas into the useful shale,
we'll go fishing for electricity,
we'll run out of names by the final gale.

47

This place, which another piety built,
is now made holy with herb and twisted root
and grassy odour and a bird's summer lilt,
some flighty piccolo, some living, far-off flute,
unheard by the enraged, or the pacified,
and outside today's crack-pot, moonlit mind,
this church, whatever it once deified,
the rot of time has not yet undermined,
now, what the long-dead raised to heaven
has since become a testament in lichen,
and by sun and rain long overwritten
in blue and green to efface all religion.
Not far, just past the railway lines,
where new and dingy streets are satisfactory
for obviously bad omens from triple climes,
behold, a polymer plastics factory!

48

An ever unwinding wind over the pathless mountains,
chilled by glacier and the sheer and dizzying steep,
reaches the pale stems and shakes free their grains,
which the fragile moon wakes from shallow sleep
to fill neglected fields with silvery wheat
(beneath the icy stars this vast winter harvest
will never make any locust man replete).
With such uncalled-for abundance is idle chance blessed.
Now wander, rare soul, to the calamitous shore
where among the countless waves of the boundless sea
the black river uncoils to be no more
and see how very full the void can be.

49

Alive with the winds of aerial physiognomy
a cloud, sunlit pink, smiles and beckons
from beyond the hypnotised turquoise sea
forever and ever, not just for so many seconds.
Now, to be eternal, as I think, is to be wise,
yet asked for wisdom, the cloud replies,

'Time is a big, old ticking clock,
'ticking because it cannot stop,
'and the world is a lump of flying rock,
'flying because it cannot drop,
'but if it were to drop, I would not fear,
'because I should never stop floating here.'

On the daily watch for degeneracy
one even envies the pure fresh air
that glides beyond that turquoise sea,
to be the living blank who caresses her there,
the inverse of a soul, yet likewise deathless,
as empty headed, but never breathless.

50

The mystery of what I am
may be answered by nothing at all
and the issue of any man
is another man, another flaw.

Errors and horrors prior to oblivion
result in a war memorial arboretum,
more concrete to rap their heels upon.
Heels and leaves that fly in autumn.

Although this has happened before,
it will begin again, if anything can,
and nothing's answered after all
about the mystery of what I am.

51

There are heroes, but no hero can live the winter through,
uncloaked and famished in the icy air, as sparrows do,
no, the new superman must abide in the snow
as mighty as the garden sparrow.

There are heroes, but there are no heroes without a tale
and yet many tales are told and they always stale,
no, the new superman best not leave the house
and stay as silent as the mouse.

There are heroes, but in time no hero stays whole,
flesh loosens into parts, nothing like the soul,
no, the new superman must consist
of what's not certain to exist.

52

Easier to believe in the forbidden tree
as their rule grows authoritarian,
their law, ever more arbitrary,
thus God, when we were agrarian,
what fruits were proscribed, but not why,
it was a tyrant's typical whim,
and we were watched by the supple spy,
one coiled around every green limb,
because apples bring death and sin,
the cherry's ecstasy is heresy,
and peaches and dissent are akin,
while apricots, they taste of apostasy!

53

Who cast the broken cakes between the tombs
while winter birds piped from privet and yew?
Who listened, as if to voices in next-door rooms,
to hear what lies beyond murder, or flu?

Is the necromancer out and about
dressed like the average man in the street?
Is he more or less doubting, or devote,
for dancing on the sexton's six feet?

Not for us what is patently obscene,
to teach famished bones to sit up and dine,
yet who doesn't feed some yellow-faced machine
in the hope of learning we are divine?

54

If God is real, then we are unreal,
cartoon swine for the great abattoir,
I.O.U.s from life's common weal;
unreal, we and death are on a par.
If we are real, then God cannot exist,
there is no room in the shifting pattern
that atoms make, for only atoms persist,
the rest is a vacuum spirit cannot fatten.
If we are real, then nothing matters,
except transcendence, that is, to divest
ourselves of these tatters
and ease the fretful mind that cannot rest,
that rook's nest, so hard to wear, our crown,
as maddened kings of a solid state,
an empire of the known unknown.
If only we might abdicate!

55

Could there have ever been a sleeping giant within,
one who wore the polar star instead of the tin
and took a call to vocation from an electrocuted tree
and served fish in Paris trawled from the *Haunted Sea*?

Could a prodigy have worn this small, derided frame,
endured this small-time luck, borne this common name,
watched each act of self defeat and every mistake,
and still not thought himself, after all, a dreadful fake?

56

The faithful are reciting the blackest books.
O prophets, you are growing bolder!
In cold fields, startled by a flock of rooks,
I see your bombs will burst the fouler.

Athwart wind blasts the ploughed
earth of a final, but oppressive autumn.
Hear! Bellowing desert men grow more loud,
but final spring comes when all is dumb.

For now, listen to the lowing of the kine
presaging an alteration of the beast,
and corralled by the electric line,
they cry, "You're still not us, at least."

That even bombs, will one day moulder
and a flock of squalling rooks
will sit on your bones, O you prophets, the bolder,
is not written in your blackest books.

57

Along the intestines of the jungle,
in the plastic and sewage-filled rivers,
where nature is free to bungle,
bad luck finally delivers.
And from there it's imported,
this little box of monkey tricks
(its crimes so far unreported)
into our paradise of parallel bricks.

58

I saw an eagle buzzed by a gull and rook,
which sight I have never seen before,
and thought of *All-in Fighting,* a book
I bought because it's already war.

I sat in the overgrown garden
of the dead couple next door,
dead of old age, one Sunday, at ten,
listening to the gunning traffic roar.

The village pedo, black beard
and square, black-rimmed glasses,
the dictator look, so will he be feared
soon, as now by children's asses?

Below the hill I saw the dented tin,
once full of extra-strength beer,
discharged, but it missed the bin,
and floats now at the sewage weir.

Pointing from the rubbish skip, a scanner
(a winnowed Christmas pine)
detected the enemy's radio yammer
within the wind's whistle and whine.

Yes, and that utter streak of piss,
Aaron, who stacks shelves at the store,
will be told, *A machine can do all this,
but opportunity knocks. It's war!*

59

So what monster? What bloated stomach
vomited all this up, so unclean, so unkind,
nasty molecules, running amok,
going so far as to frame a soulless mind?
So what monster staled this river
of urine, now flooding the gutter,
(the municipal river Lethe)
into which the senile mutter?
So what monster, excremental
decreed the very nature of our meat
is just as providential
as some mongrel's feast in the street?

60

There are far, far too many signs,
a map entirely of parallel lines
and hung at dawn, a guilty spider
weaves the polygon ever wider
for the beast of countless names
and tomorrow's oven flames.

61

Fuck off memory,
how I hate the past!
I want no summary.
Scrub it, first to last.
Those to come, be none,
you, old chums, be gone.

62

Under planet Saturn's lowest ebb
spring-sown seeds came to their head,
but now that aerial, the dew-filled web,
is downward bent, because it's for lead
to draw everything dainty to the ground,
from the grass stalks to the faintest cloud
and under Saturn the falling leaves resound,
while the shades stand in a silent crowd
to watch the little beasts' sacrifice,
the flighty sparrows and trembling mice,
interred now below the yew, edifice
holy for those who do not live twice.
Now we, for whom the future is fear,
expect the return of another year.

63

A spring morning and the lawn mowers drone
today … nothing's so far away as today,
tomorrow robots will settle in the home,
Tomorrow? Why, that's almost today,
so, what will you do, O *tomorrow fellow*?
Wait for the lawn to be mown
watching a screen, listening to the bellow
of a simian snout at a megaphone?
Well, know but for the doorman and harlot
and philosopher whispering alone
and criminals who can't be forgot,
you, *today fellow*, will become unknown.

64

Because of the bridge in the woods I know
about the stream tumbling from the hill and, below
that hill, the standing mist and, at the other end,
the living pool, over which three yew trees bend.
Long since begun at the new scavengers' feast
the silent presidency of the most ominous beast,
fur and feathers, rain blackened and thick,
who observes which mortal path you pick,
either to follow the course of the stream,
or to cross the bridge, but only in a dream,
and leave all else to the day of slaughter
and alone breathe the mist, or drink the water,
as the beast ordains, without sign or sound,
or both together, or the other way round.

65

If this all-too-busy earth has a skull
composed of rock with a magnetic pull,
dead, unlike its skin of plant and creature,
though this is a temporary feature
in spite of everything that is done,
the future's the head of a skeleton,
and to the sun the skull will turn and turn
until the sun has nothing left to burn,
then off it has to fly, into the void,
just one more eyeless asteroid.

66

The cone, its point simple and indivisible,
therefore never subject to decay, it is the soul.
The circle is everything that is not null,
its infinite opposites make the whole.

Cones rid of nature fill the Apollonian
books, ellipse of moth and arc of frog,
without rancid pond or flickering neon,
described without time's spring and cog.

Might I, tangentially set,
hop and flutter mechanically through
the clockwork of matter to yet
come to the eternal point with you?

67

Come sweet post-mortem grace,
the day is done, there is no trace,
of man to hear the sirens' song
sung by forest winds all night long,
nor, by beams from silver moon,
to see autumn's silken cocoon
nor, reborn, moths in the sky
never by false light to die,
or rivers fly, or mountains fall,
or roofs shake when birds call,
and no decay, no disgrace,
O come sweet post-mortem grace!

68

He brushed the whispering leaves down the tiled hallway and out through the front door, adding them to the heap in the middle of the road. A frozen veil of fog had draped herself over the street of Victorian redbrick houses, which exhibited both the grandeur and desolation of giant mausoleums. And then the bare poplar trees, stationed along the empty pavements, seemed to him like the tall, fleshless brides of concentration-camp weddings. They held their black bouquets high up against the smouldering sky as if to fling them over the rooftops, Concealed in the gardens, the waiting bridesmaids were dying to settle the question of who would be the next to wed. *Whooooo...?* Behind him, a tin skull whistled between its teeth. *Wheeeeeshshshooo!* He started from his daydream and the tall brides turned back into wood. Hurrying back through the house and into the kitchen, he snatched the singing kettle off its nest of snivelling gas. He hated the thin whine of the steam whistle and reproached himself for allowing the silence of the dead world to be broken. He gazed at the vapour rising from the spout and wondered if it had woken anyone in the great cloudy sphere on which he lived. Perhaps some ghost would rise from the depths of a dusty mirror, or from behind a pair of lost spectacles. Perhaps it would come calling soon. So, having set the tea to brew, he set out two cups and two saucers, just in case.

69

...

INDEX OF FIRST LINES

Ah, a professional numerator	21
Adam and his Siamese twin, Eve	7
Alive with the winds of aerial physiognomy	30
All are types and each is loved	7
Allow me to tell you, as evening advances	6
Along the intestines of the jungle	34
An ever unwinding wind over the pathless mountains	29
At the very last rank of quiescent night	25
Autobiography by non anon	21
Because of the bridge in the woods I know	38
Behold the monsters, on the street	18
Beyond the skeleton stilts and sheets of flesh	27
Come sweet post-mortem grace	39
Could there have ever been a sleeping giant within	33
Dawn, and they sound so overjoyed	13
Dear God, not yet another provincial bore	22
Despite the brooding clouds saying who knows what	15
Easier to believe in the forbidden tree	32

Exotic animals in cages	11
Fuck off memory	35
Give to the King of the Dead	16
God damn this provincial hole	22
God help me, I want a war	15
Hail prophet, whose prophecies have never dimmed	24
He brushed the whispering leaves down the tiled hallway	40
I saw an eagle buzzed by a gull and rook	35
I see the future in electric cables	8
If God is real, then we are unreal	33
In this age of ever more infectious crimes	28
Last night the stars never shone so far away	24
Let all the graveyards join as one place	19
Let the flags of the future unfold and fold	22
Let them speak six times a hour	10
Look, nature is a host of fanatics	27
Lord, it seems yours is the greater sway	20
Not born deformed, to grovel in a chair?	8
On the day the Earth stands still	20
Our aim was swift and true	17
So many, so many, like leaves of trees	12

So what monster? What bloated stomach	36
The banana falls not far from the banana tree	14
The cone, its point simple and indivisible	39
The faithful are reading the blackest books	34
The hill resonates with arrows of geese	26
The index, that obituary of a book	40
The ivied-wooded ways, sacred to the moon	24
The mystery of what I am	31
The prim whores, the labouring drones	5
The same rain on the bare-browed hills	37
The universe is a dirty plaster wall	9
The world ended last night	5
There are far, far too many signs	35
There are heroes, but no hero can live the winter through	31
There's crucial fish in our lavatory sea	28
These things in our heads aren't memories	10
This all-too-busy earth has a skull	38
This is the night where my heart longs to quicken	12
This place, which another piety built	29
To converse with them is hardly worthwhile	19
Trees and trees and trees will grow	25

Turn the tap, fill the swimming pool with blood	21
Under planet Saturn's lowest ebb	37
We are surrounded by things that live at our command	26
What a world of amity	18
What else is man? After the battle	26
Whenever you are told	14
Who left the broken cakes amongst the tombs	32
You ask, *What are these days?* These are the last days	9

DETATCHED TITLES

The Covenant. I See the Future. Diarrhoeic Revelation. The New Superman. The Virus. What Monster? Under Saturn. Spectral Lives. The Little Witness. Hollywood Zoo. The Serpent's Bliss. Blessings. Reverse Elegy. The New Prophet. Junky Star. Necromancers. The Same Rain Here. World War Three. The Harvest. Look! The Problem with Matter. New Year's Day. The Plague. Alien Hero. Unmasked Shadow. Spiteful Redeemer. The Arithmetical Mediation. Bad Ideas. Sigh Monotone Breeze. Ten Thousand Stars Off. Where Fanfare No Bees. No Hymns Whispers Moth. Shine Ten Thousand Days. Blaze All Tomorrow. Rise Many Milky Ways. Blot Out Black Sorrow. Solstice Wind. The Light in Anniversary Silver. What Bible? Turning Once in Century These Mills. Grind the Flour for My Bread. Older than all the hills. The Glass of Wine. Beside My Bed. Snow that Fell from a Sky of Black Long Before the Stars were Started. Still Covers the Fields and Chimney Stack. Of My Land. Never to be Charted. Broken Cakes. Just in Case. The Skies Counted. Nobody Listens to. Those Around You. Time and Tide. Innocent Prime. Unquenchable Dream. Invisible Stream. Life Made Plain. Wind and Rain. Holes in the Sky. God's Peering Eye. Self Defeating Acts. Inheritance Tax. Rose at Dawn. Men and Days Grow Faint. Massive Fraction. Sexton's Six Feet. Another Flaw. Teach Yourself Mechanics by P Abbott. The Sheperd is a Scarecrow.

The Golem

Behold the dream that did not settle,
but rose at dawn to walk by day
with teeth of precious metal
and limbs of rust-streaked clay
wetted with tears and fired by grief
before this spell to make him start
I set behind his golden teeth:
Go and tear the world apart.

My Saint

A streetlight shines where the sun might rise, tomorrow,
and the holy fool (but honest) might deny you know
whether or not another light will ever shine
for an eternal night, quiet and blessed and all mine,
or, when the memory of men and days grow faint,
that I would lapse, that I would not revere my saint.

www.ingramcontent.com/pod-product-compliance
Lightning Source LLC
Chambersburg PA
CBHW020549080526
44583CB00013B/1065